D0605190

SCARD

eXtreme Games

Winter Action Sports

Jim Brush

SEA-TO-SEA

Mankato Collingwood London

This edition first published in 2013 by

Sea-to-Sea Publications
Distributed by Black Rabbit Books
P.O. Box 3263, Mankato, Minnesota 56002

Copyright © Sea-to-Sea Publications 2013

Printed in the United States of America,
North Mankato, MN.

All rights reserved.

9 8 7 6 5 4 3 2

Published by arrangement with the Watts
Publishing Group Ltd, London.

A CIP catalog record is available from the
Library of Congress.

ISBN: 978-1-59771-408-2

Series Editor: Adrian Cole
Art Director: Jonathan Hair
Design: Graham Rich Design
Picture Research: Diana Morris

The X-Games logo is the property of ESPN,
Inc. CORPORATION DELAWARE, ESPN Plaza,
Bristol, CONNECTICUT 06010. This product is
not endorsed by ESPN, Inc.

Acknowledgments:

Richard Bord/Getty Images: 23, 32, 40.
Bo Bridges/Corbis: front cover. Jean-Pierre
Clatot/AFP/Getty Images: 15, 42, 43.
Jessica Goodman/Getty Images: 8. Jonathan
Moore/Getty Images: 41. Doug Pensinger/
Getty Images: 4, 6, 10, 11, 12, 13, 14, 16,
17, 19, 21, 26, 30, 33, 35, 38. Christian
Pondella/Getty Images: 2, 7, 9, 20, 24, 27,
31, 36, 37. Quinn Rooney/Getty Images: 39.
Kristy Sparow/Getty Images: 22, 34. Jamie
Squire/Getty Images: 28-29. Olav Stubberud,
www.olavstubberud.com: 18.

Every attempt has been made to clear copyright.
Should there be any inadvertent omission please
apply to the publisher for rectification.

RD/6000006415/001
May 2012

Contents

Words highlighted in the text can be found in the glossary.

Welcome to the X-Games

In the Winter X-Games, the world's top winter sports athletes compete to perform the best tricks and earn the fastest times in the quest for X-Games gold. The winter sports competition showcases snowboarding, snowmobile racing, and skiing.

The Winter X-Games are held every year and attract more than 200 athletes from around the world. Gold, silver, and bronze medals, as well as prize money, are up for grabs.

Snowboarder Shaun White flies through the air during X-Games 14 in 2010. He went on to claim gold in the SuperPipe event.

With a sensational stunt, Levi LaVallee demonstrates why snowmobile racing has become a crowd favorite.

The "X" in Winter X-Games stands for extreme. The games are the place for diehard winter sports stars to show off their most spectacular stunts. In 2006, snowboarder Jeaux Hall tried and failed 17 times before landing the world's first **1080** (three spins in the air). His fellow competitors urged him on from the sidelines. It's all part of the spirit of the games.

eXtreme fact

Being an action sports star requires guts. Take snowboarder Scotty Lago: in the 2011 Winter X-Games, he competed in the SuperPipe competition with a broken jaw—and won silver!

Where's the Action?

Over the years, several of the USA's top ski resorts have been used to host the Winter X-Games. In 2010, a new X-Games winter competition was held in Europe for the first time.

The mountains of Big Bear Lake, California.

eXtreme fact

In 1997, Sweden's Jennie Waara became the only athlete in Winter X-Games history to win three medals in the same year: Snowboarder X gold, Halfpipe silver, and Slopestyle bronze.

The first Winter X-Games ever took place in January 1997, at the Snow Summit Mountain Resort in Big Bear Lake, California. Athletes competed in ice climbing, snow BMX racing, and Moto X, as well as snowboarding. One of the big stars was Norwegian snowboarder Daniel Franck, nicknamed the "Slippery Hotdog," who took gold in men's Slopestyle and silver in the **Halfpipe** event.

Snocross action from Buttermilk Mountain during X-Games 14 held in 2010.

From 1998–9, the X-Games were held in Crested Butte Mountain Resort, in Colorado. Here, fans watched new sports, such as stunt, or "Free," skiing, SkiBoarding, and snowmobile racing. Since 2002, the Winter X-Games have taken place at Buttermilk Mountain in Aspen, Colorado. Today, more than 80,000 fans attend five days of awesome events.

eXtreme fact

In 2004, the Winter X-Games were televized live for the first time. In 2009, clips of Winter X-Games stars such as Shaun White were made into a stunning 3-D movie.

On the Edge

Rising action sports stars often get their first big break at the X-Games. Here they are encouraged to take risks and to be the first to do a new trick.

Competitors push themselves hard, but if they take a tumble, the other competitors encourage them to try again. There's always the danger of getting injured, but star status awaits if they can pull off a monster stunt!

Torin Yater-Wallace competing in the Men's Skiing SuperPipe at X-Games 15.

eXtreme fact

In 2011, 15-year-old Torin Yater-Wallace became the youngest winner of a Winter X-Games skiing medal when he earned silver in the Ski SuperPipe event. He beat competitors 10 years older than him!

Canadian Ashleigh McIvor (in green) flies over a jump in the Women's Skier X event.

The 2011 Winter X-Games were marked by several big crashes. Attempting a **grab**, Jacob Webster ripped off his ski in midair during the Big **Air** event, and slammed onto the ramp. Skier Simon Dumont had a bone-crunching smash onto the **lip** of the SuperPipe, while Olympic gold medalist Ashleigh McIvor had to be carried off on a stretcher after injuring her knee in the Women's Skier X event.

eXtreme fact

Levi LaVallee tried the first double **backflip** on a snowmobile in the 2009 Freestyle Snocross event. He landed it, and became an instant X-Games legend.

Snowboarding Action

Snowboarding has become a hugely popular sport at the Winter X-Games. This is largely thanks to a group of snowboarders in Lake Tahoe, California. They created the first halfpipe in the 1980s.

Nic Suave rides a rail during a practice run for the Snowboard Street event in 2011.

eXtreme fact

In Snowboard Street, athletes compete in a 30-minute **jam** session, hitting urban obstacles such as giant rails. Nic Suave won the first ever event in 2011.

Today, professional or "pro" snowboarders have developed hundreds of new skills and stunts. At the Winter X-Games, snowboarders get to show off their best tricks in events such as SuperPipe, Slopestyle, Big Air, and Snowboard Street.

In snowboarding, known as "**shredding,**" injuries are common. The competitors wear a range of gear to protect themselves, especially in the Big Air event. This includes: helmets; padding on hips, knees, spine, and shoulders; and goggles.

eXtreme fact

Another new event at the Winter X-Games from 2011 was Real Snow. Eight of the best riders in the world are judged on 60-second video clips. These show them **grinding** down long rails and shooting jumps across massive gaps.

Modern snowboards are made from a wooden core, surrounded by **fiberglass** with steel edges. Many pros use the same freestyle board for the SuperPipe and Slopestyle events. These are short and flexible. The boards used in Snowboarder X are built for speed. They are long, narrow, and stiff.

Elena Hight grabs some air during the Women's Snowboard SuperPipe event. Her freestyle board has curved, turned-up ends.

SuperPipe Dreams

The Halfpipe is a classic snowboarding event. In 2001, the X-Games went one better—creating the awesome SuperPipe event.

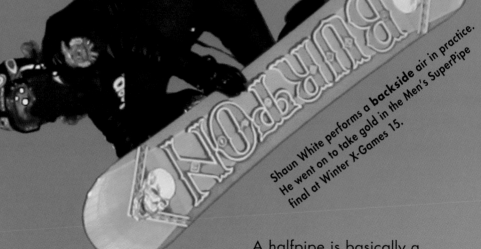

Shaun White performs a **backside** air in practice. He went on to take gold in the Men's SuperPipe final at Winter X-Games 15.

eXtreme fact

The X-Games SuperPipe at Aspen is 568 feet (173 m) long. Pro snowboarders can pull off five or six tricks on a course this long.

A halfpipe is basically a U-shaped tube on a downward slope. The SuperPipe is a steeper, bigger version of this, some 23 feet (7 m) deep. This allows snowboarders to get maximum height—or "big air"—above the frozen ground. Competitors link a run of amazing aerial tricks together. The judges look for big air, good style, and perfect landings, and observe how everything flows together.

Landing a move that no one else can do is a great way of getting the judges' attention in the SuperPipe event. In the 2011 Winter X-Games, snowboarder Kelly Clark became the first woman to land a 1080 in a contest.

Kelly Clark flies high during the Women's SuperPipe final.

In 2010, Shaun White unveiled his impossibly hard Double McTwist 12—two flips and three-and-a-half spins. Though the trick helped him to win gold, he famously smashed his face on the lip of the SuperPipe while trying out the move in training.

eXtreme fact

In 2011, Shaun White set a new SuperPipe record by winning four gold medals in four consecutive years.

So Smooth Slopestyle

The Slopestyle course tests a boarder's ability to handle all kinds of different features. It's all about doing a variety of stylish tricks while getting good height off the jumps.

The Slopestyle event is performed on specially made trails at ski mountains. These "**jib** parks" are filled with various jumps, boxes, and other obstacles.

The Slopestyle park includes:

• Jib rails, in all shapes and sizes
• Boxes—these are sometimes buses or barrels buried in the snow!
• Joy sticks: poles with a big ball stuck on top.

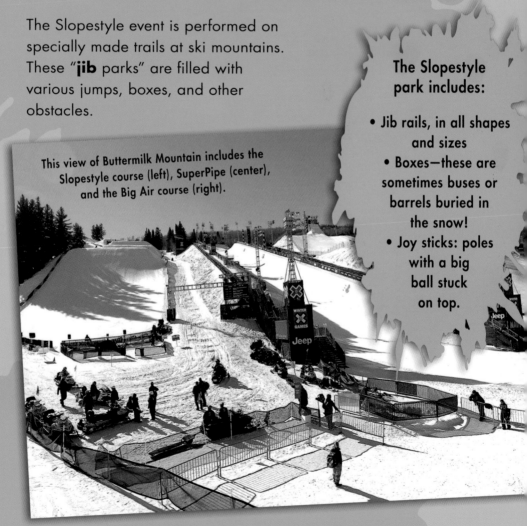

This view of Buttermilk Mountain includes the Slopestyle course (left), SuperPipe (center), and the Big Air course (right).

The best Slopestyle boarders flow from trick to trick to make their run look smooth and effortless. These include spins, grabs, grinds, and flips.

In 2011, at the Winter X-Games Europe Slopestyle event, Chas Guldemond achieved a 99.33 out of a possible 100! This was the highest score achieved by anyone in the competition.

Sage Kotsenburg on a jib rail during practice for the Slopestyle event.

In 2009, Jenny Jones' Snowboard Slopestyle win made her the first female Winter X-Games medalist from Great Britain. She won the following year as well in the USA and Europe!

Big Air and Snowboarder X

The crowd-pleasing Big Air event is a chance for the biggest names in freestyle snowboarding to show off their craziest stunts while flying across a huge 85-foot (26-m) gap!

This sequence photograph shows Torstein Horgmo jumping in the Big Air practice.

The 2011 event summed up what Big Air is all about. Norwegian snowboarder Torstein Horgmo stepped up for this third attempt at "The Triple," the world's first triple corkscrew. He was suffering from two broken ribs, having fallen hard on his two previous attempts. But with the crowd screaming him on, he soared off the ramp, flipped three times in the air, and landed the trick.

eXtreme fact

In a Snowboarder X semifinal in 2010, world champion snowboarder Max Schairer of Austria had to be taken to the hospital after a nasty collision with two other boarders.

Snowboardercross, or Snowboarder X, is a mix between snowboarding and Moto X. Six boarders race head-to-head down a course 3,600 feet (1,097 m) long, snaking around tight turns and over jumps. All the time they are looking for places to pass. First down to the bottom wins!

Accidents—or **wipeouts**—in Snowboarder X are common. More injuries occur in Snowboarder X than almost any other event at the Winter X-Games.

Seth Wescott (center) leads the way in the X-Games 15 Men's Snowboarder X.

Snowboard Stars

In its short history, the Winter X-Games has been dominated by snowboarding sensations such as Shaun White and Lindsey Jacobellis.

Shaun White

American Shaun White is one of a kind. He has won a medal at the Winter X-Games every year since 2002, including 17 golds and 11 other medals by 2011. In 2009, he captured his fourth straight Slopestyle title, then in 2011 pulled off the same feat in the SuperPipe event. His red hair and fancy airborne moves earned him the nickname the "Flying Tomato!"

Shaun White holds up his snowboard to the crowd after winning gold in the Men's Snowboarding SuperPipe in January 2011.

eXtreme fact

In 2007, Shaun White became the first person to win a gold medal at both the Summer and Winter X-Games.

Lindsey Jacobellis displays her gold medal after her win in the Women's Snowboarder X, in 2011.

Lindsey Jacobellis

"Lucky" Lindsey Jacobellis first entered the X-Games at the age of 15 and has won the Snowboarder X gold an incredible seven times, including a run of four victories in a row. Jacobellis is also known for her great attitude. She famously lost out on Snowboarder X Olympic Gold after she crash-landed on the next-to-last jump trying a fancy move. She said afterward, "I was just having fun, and I messed up."

eXtreme fact

In 2006, unstoppable Slopestyle competitor Janna Meyen-Weatherby became the first Winter X-Games athlete ever to **four-peat** in a single event.

Let's Party!

The atmosphere at the X-Games is very special. As well as death-defying stunts, there are live music events at the X Fest, celebrity spectators, and competitions for fans.

Competitors gather at a press conference for the Winter X-Games.

eXtreme fact

Mono skier Josh Dueck summed up the spirit of the X-Games: "It's a community feel. Everybody is working with each other to make sure that everyone has their best performance and they put on a good show."

Tens of thousands of fans turn Aspen into one big party for the X-Games—despite the freezing weather! The X-Games last for five days, and they're free. Screaming fans can watch several events at once on monster-sized TV screens.

In the Snowskate Park, young fans get the chance to show off their skills on rails and ledges, or try out the latest gear. There's also the chance to meet the stars face-to-face and get their autograph. Some fans wear T-shirts over their winter coats, covered in athletes' signatures!

eXtreme fact

In 2002, 380 out of 470 students failed to show up for school when the X-Games was first staged in the resort. Since then, Aspen's school students are given the Friday of the X-Games off.

Skier Kevin Rolland signs autographs for waiting extreme sports fans.

Sled Mayhem

Snowmobiles, also known as sleds, are capable of eye-popping stunts, 100-foot (30-m) leaps—and truly spectacular crashes. All in all, a perfect match for the Winter X-Games!

Modern snowmobiles are fast and powerful. They can reach speeds of 75 miles (120 km) per hour or more in under four seconds. They are popular with fans because the riders perform incredible stunts.

Snowmobile racing made its first appearance at the Winter X-Games in 1998, followed by the Freestyle, and Speed & Style competitions.

Riders wear a wide range of protective gear including:

- Helmet
- Gloves
- Goggles
- Leather boots
- Shin and knee guards
- Elbow pads
- Neck braces

Snowmobile riders face extreme dangers. Imagine one of those heavy, bone-crunching machines landing on top of you! In 2011, medal favorite Heath Frisby crashed out of the Freestyle event when his right arm slipped out of the hold. This made his body twist and he was ripped off the sled.

eXtreme fact

Snowmobile events can be dangerous for officials, too! During the Snocross finals in 2011, Bobby LePage's snowmobile flew off the course after a bumpy landing. It crashed into official Val Meyer, knocking him off his feet.

Levi LaVallee during practice for the Freestyle snowmobile competition.

Crazy Flipping Freestyle

Snowmobile Freestyle is one of the most jaw-dropping events of the whole X-Games. Bulky 450-pound (205-kg) machines doing backflips in the snow has to be seen to be believed!

Justin Hoyer kicks out in midair in the Freestyle event at Winter X-Games 15.

Freestyle snowmobile riders, nicknamed "sled necks," can make the tricks look easy. But they risk their lives every time their machines take off into the air, especially when doing upside-down or "inverted" stunts.

eXtreme fact

To add to the thrills, athletes don't have to say in advance what stunt they are going to perform. Fans never know what is coming next.

In the Freestyle event, the judges look for runs that are smooth and controlled. In 2009, the left ski on Justin Hoyer's machine landed just outside the jump area. It cost him gold—though he came back to win the event in 2010.

The Next Trick competition sees snowmobile riders performing their biggest stunts. In 2010, Heath Frisby won gold with his Tsunami flip (above), in which he "ran" beneath his upside-down sled in midair!

eXtreme fact

For years, Caleb Moore had raced all-terrain vehicles. In December 2009, he switched from wheels to skis. Incredibly, just a month later he won bronze in the Winter X-Games Snowmobile Freestyle event!

Snocross and Speed & Style

Snocross is all-out snowmobile racing. The racers compete on tracks made up of tight turns, banked corners, steep jumps, and obstacles.

The competition is always fierce in Snocross. The first courses were longer, with deeper holes and higher jumps. Modern courses are built for speed. Even so, the jumps are up to 30 feet (9 m) high, making the riders soar up to 130 feet (40 m) before landing again—with a thump.

The start is all-important, because the winner is often quickest through the first turn, known as the "**holeshot.**" Once they get going, the sleds can reach speeds of up to 60 miles (97 km) per hour.

Snowmobile Speed & Style combines the air of Freestyle and the speed of Snocross in a single event. Pairs of competitors zoom around the course hitting side-by-side ramps. After four laps of racing, the rider who crosses the finish line first wins the speed portion. But the rider finishing second can still win if his style score is high enough to make up the difference.

Riders accelerate away from the starting line in a Snocross competition.

eXtreme fact

In 2011, a new Snocross event was included in the Winter X-Games—Adaptive Snocross. This ran on the Snocross course, with a few changes, to suit snowmobile riders with disabilities. American Mike Schultz won gold.

Snowmobile Monsters

The stars of the snowmobile events have provided many unforgettable moments, such as Aleksander Nordgaard's record-breaking 105-foot (32-m) backflip in the Freestyle event in 2007.

Tucker Hibbert

In 2000, Hibbert defeated reigning champion Blair Morgan, a five-times X-Games gold medalist whose stand-up, high-flying style changed the sport forever. Hibbert went on to dominate the sport, winning a remarkable five golds in a row from 2007 to 2011.

eXtreme fact

Tucker Hibbert won gold in the 2000 Snocross event at just 15, becoming the youngest gold medalist in Winter X-Games history.

Tucker Hibbert flying to victory in the Snocross competition at X-Games 15.

Swedish star Daniel Bodin won the Freestyle and Best Trick events in 2011.

Daniel Bodin

In 2011, Daniel Bodin performed the first ever Double Grab flip. He has appeared in the snowmobile Freestyle event every year since it was added to the X-Games in 2007.

Levi LaVallee

Freestyler Levi LaVallee first made the headlines when he won two gold medals at the 2008 Winter X-Games. The next year, he became the first person in history to attempt a double backflip in competition.

eXtreme fact

Some of the top freestyle riders train in indoor foam pits to keep their newest tricks hidden from other competitors. The foam also gives them a softer landing!

Preparing the Course

Preparation for a Winter X-Games event starts a long time before the athletes and fans show up at the venue.

This Snow Cat is fitted with a 21-foot (6.4-m) high Zaugg Pipe Monster.

A lot of work goes into building the various courses. All of the snow features for the Winter X-Games, such as the SuperPipe, jumps, and giant **moguls**, are sculpted from machine-made snow. Special vehicles, called Snow Cats, scoop snow into position. Then huge arms, called Pipe Monsters, are used to shape the curved sides of the SuperPipe.

eXtreme fact

Snow machines turn water into tiny droplets using a jet of high-pressure air. When the droplets are blown into freezing air, they become snow crystals.

Every course has to be just right to get the very best out of the competitors. A laser measure is used to check the curve of the SuperPipe slope. The Slopestyle course changes every year. It takes 10 days or more to build it. Snow ramps are created, and rails and boxes are put into place.

This is part of the Winter X-Games course at Buttermilk Mountain. The Snowboard Street course is at the front, with the snowmobile course behind it.

Freestyle Skiing

Mind-blowing stunts performed by freestyle skiers at the Winter X-Games have raised the profile of skiing. It's now just as cool as snowboarding.

There were no skiing events at the first Winter X-Games in 1997. But around this time, **twin-tip** skis became available. Their turned-up tips and tails allowed skiers to perform stunts backward, or "**fakie.**" Soon skiers were performing jumps, grabs, and grinds just like snowboarders.

Canadian Justin Dorey catches some air off the SuperPipe.

eXtreme fact

In 2007, Peter Olenick performed the first ever double-flip in the Skiing SuperPipe event. Nicknamed the "Whisky Flip," it led to a new era of even more amazing tricks.

Freestyle skiing became part of the X-Games in 1998. The first Big Air event was held a year later. This was followed by Slopestyle and SuperPipe in 2002. Since then, freestyle skiing has continued to grow, thanks to **pioneers** like Tanner Hall and John Olsson.

Simon Dumont on his X-Games gold medal-winning run in 2004.

The Skiing SuperPipe competition takes place on the same giant U-shaped pipe as the snowboarding event. Every year the stunts get bigger and better. In 2004, Simon Dumont rose 22 feet (6.7 m) above the deck to win Skiing SuperPipe gold.

Skiing Big Air and Slopestyle

The Winter X-Games showcases the most exciting freestyle skiers in the world. The Skiing Big Air and Slopestyle events are a feast of crazy flips and spins.

Bobby Brown almost disappears into the night sky during the Ski Big Air event.

The Big Air event has always been one of the biggest crowd-pullers. In the 2010 event, T. J. Schiller landed the first double corked 1620 ever—that's four-and-a-half spins in the air. Unbelievably, it wasn't enough to win gold! In only his second Winter X-Games, 18-year-old Bobby Brown stepped up and achieved a perfect score of 100, performing two tricks that had never been landed before in competition.

Kaya Turski launches down the start ramps on the Ski Slopestyle course.

eXtreme fact

Canadian skier Kaya Turski won the first Women's Slopestyle Skiing competition in 2010, with the highest Slopestyle score ever at a Winter X-Games of 96.66.

In the Slopestyle event, skiers combine big air and technical tricks into one run. They follow the same course as snowboarders, combining spins, grabs, grinds, and flips.

The judges score highly for style and control. In the 2011 event, many competitors had trouble with the fast Slopestyle course. But after all three runs, Sammy Carlson took gold in the men's competition.

Downhill Dynamos

Skier X and Mono Skier X are more like traditional downhill skiing events. But there's no shortage of drama as four competitors race head-to-head on a fast and furious course.

Kelsey Serwa (above) crashes down with Ophelie David (top right) during the Women's Skier X final.

The Skier X, or Skicross, course combines steep slopes with jumps and gates. Though pushing and pulling are banned, spectacular collisions add to the thrills. In the 2011 Women's event, Kelsey Serwa and Ophelie David were neck-and-neck at the last jump. They got tangled during the landing and wiped out. Luckily for Serwa, she slid across the finish line first and won gold.

Mono Skier X features mono skiers with disabilities racing over tabletop jumps, banked turns, rollers, and gaps. Like Skier X, there are lots of crashes and wipeouts. In the 2011 final, two out of four skiers fell. The final jump is huge, with skiers leaping 82 feet (25 m) or more.

eXtreme fact

In 2011, veteran mono skier Chris Devlin-Young became the oldest athlete to compete at the Winter X-Games, age 49.

Josh Dueck won gold in the Mono Skier X in 2011.

Skiing Supremos

There's no shortage of skiing superstars at the Winter X-Games.

Tanner Hall

Tanner Hall is probably the biggest name in Freestyle skiing. He earned his first Winter X-Games gold in 2001. By 2008, he had become the only person to "three-peat" in two Winter X-Games events, adding three straight Skiing SuperPipe wins to his Slopestyle victories.

eXtreme fact

In 2005, doctors said Tanner Hall might never ski again after breaking both ankles jumping over the notorious 118-foot (36-m) wide Chad's Gap in the wilds of Utah. It didn't stop Hall from claiming gold at the X-Games Superpipe the next year!

Simon Dumont

With eight X-Games under his belt, Simon Dumont (above) is best known for his great height in the SuperPipe competitions. In 2008, he became the world record holder for the highest ski air on a **quarterpipe**, at 35 feet (10.7 m).

Sarah Burke

Canadian skier Sarah Burke won her fourth gold medal in the Women's SuperPipe competition in 2011. Sadly, Sarah died as a result of injuries sustained in an accident in January 2012.

Ophelie David

French skier Ophelie David (above) is the queen of Skier X, winning gold four years in a row from 2007 to 2010—the first skier to do this. She is also a very talented mountain biker.

X-Games Europe

In 2010, for the first time the Winter X-Games Europe (or WXE) competition took place in Tignes, in France.

Perhaps the highlight of the 2010 event was the Double McTwist **1260** landed by Swiss snowboarder Iouri Podladtchikov, known as the "I-Pod." He only began practicing the trick a week before. This gave him the gold medal in the SuperPipe with a giant score of 98.0. British snowboarder Jenny Jones also continued her winning streak in the Women's Slopestyle event by taking gold.

Norway's Kjersti Oestgaard Buaas flies high, with the winter resort of Tignes, France, in the background.

The European event was repeated the following year. Some 70,000 fans flocked to see three days of competition, with 150 athletes competing in skiing and snowboarding SuperPipe and Slopestyle events.

eXtreme fact

In 2010, a Zaugg Pipe Monster machine had to be shipped across the Atlantic to build the 720-foot (219-m) long SuperPipe course at Tignes, because it was the only machine in the world big enough.

Kevin Rolland performs an "Iron Cross" at X-Games Europe.

One of the crowd favorites at the 2011 Games was French skier Kevin Rolland, who won the SuperPipe. In the women's event, Kelly Clark claimed her third gold medal with a superb, aggressive run.

43

X-Games Medal Tables

Winter X-Games 15 (2011)	1st	2nd	3rd
Snowboarding			
Men's Slopestyle	Sebastien Toutant	Mark McMorris	Tyler Flanagan
Women's Slopestyle	Enni Rukajarvi	Jenny Jones	Jamie Anderson
Big Air	Torstein Horgmo	Sebastien Toutant	Sage Kotsenburg
Men's SuperPipe	Shaun White	Scotty Lago	Louie Vito
Women's SuperPipe	Kelly Clark	Kaitlyn Farrington	Elena Hight
Men's Snowboarder X	Nick Baumgartner	Kevin Hill	Nate Holland
Women's Snowboarder X	Lindsey Jacobellis	Callan Chythlook-Sifsof	Deborah Anthonioz
Street	Nic Sauve	Louis-Felix Paradis	Simon Chamberlain
Best Method	Scotty Lago	Ross Powers	Chas Guldemond
Snowmobile			
Freestyle	Daniel Bodin	Justin Hoyer	Caleb Moore
Speed & Style	Joe Parsons	Heath Frisby	Cory Davis
Snocross	Tucker Hibbert	Ross Martin	Robbie Malinoski
Adaptive Snocross	Mike Schultz	Jeff Tweet	Jim Wazny
Best Trick	Daniel Bodin	Caleb Moore	Heath Frisby
Skiing			
Men's Slopestyle	Sammy Carlson	Russ Henshaw	Andreas Hatvelt
Women's Slopestyle	Kaya Turski	Keri Herman	Grete Eliassen
Men's SuperPipe	Kevin Rolland	Torin Yater-Wallace	Simon Dumont
Women's SuperPipe	Sarah Burke	Brita Sigourney	Roz Groenewoud
Big Air	Alex Schlopy	Bobby Brown	Sammy Carlson
Men's Skier X	John Teller	Chris Del Bosco	Casey Puckett
Women's Skier X	Kelsey Serwa	Ophelie David	Fanny Smith
Mono Skier X	Josh Dueck	Brandon Adam	Sean Rose

Web Sites & Glossary

http://espn.go.com/action/ xgames/winter/2011
The awesome ESPN gateway to their Winter X-Games coverage, including videos, photo galleries, competitor biographies, interviews, and results, plus a cellphone app so you can stay up-to-date with everything happening on the scene, along with podcasts and Twitter feeds.

http://www.lindseyjacobellis. com/index_fl ash.html
Lindsey Jacobellis' web site featuring photos, videos, and links to her blog pages.

http://www.tucker-hibbert.com
The web site of Tucker Hibbert, which includes his biography, a photo gallery, his blog, race results, videos, and free downloadable wallpapers.

http://tannerhall.com
Tanner Hall's web site is packed with photos, movies, and competition results, along with his biography and the latest news.

Please note: Every effort has been made by the Publishers to ensure that these web sites contain no inappropriate or offensive material. However, because of the nature of the Internet, it is impossible to guarantee that the contents of these sites will not be altered. We strongly advise that Internet access is supervised by a responsible adult.

1080, 1260, 1620—Aerial spins. A complete spin is 360 degrees, so a 1080 is three spins.

Air—Short for aerial. Any time an athlete and their equipment gets airborne.

Backflip—A backward somersault in the air.

Backside—The side of a board where a snowboarder's heels sit.

Fakie—Riding backward to your normal stance.

Fiberglass—A strong, lightweight material made from various plastics strengthened by glass fibers.

Four-peat—Winning an event four times in a row. A five-peat is five wins in a row and so on.

Grab—When an athlete grabs the edge of their board, skis, or snowmobile during an aerial stunt.

Grind—Sliding along the top of an obstacle such as a rail or the lip of a ramp.

Halfpipe—The U-shaped pipe used in the X-Games Superpipe events.

Holeshot—The first corner on a Snocross racetrack.

Jam—Timed session, such as 10 minutes long, in which athletes take turns to perform stunts.

Jib—Sliding on rails or other platforms with the snowboard.

Lip—The top of a jump.

Moguls—Bumps deliberately built into a course.

Pioneers—The first people to try something out.

Quarterpipe—A single wall of the halfpipe, used in Park courses and in Big Air events.

Shredding—Slang for snowboarding down a hill.

Sled—Another name for a snowmobile.

Twin-tip—Snowboards and skis whose nose and tail are both pointed so that athletes can ride equally well in either direction.

Wipeout—A dramatic fall.

Index